My Financial Journey

*A simple step-by-step financial guide to manage
your finances with confidence and ease
throughout your lifetime.*

ANDREA ADAMS

ISBN-10: 1533124574
ISBN-13: 978-1533124579

MY FINANCIAL JOURNEY is written by ANDREA ADAMS, a graduate of the Institute for Integrative Nutrition, where they completed a cutting edge curriculum in nutrition and health coaching taught by the world's leading experts in health and wellness. I recommend you read this book and be in touch with ANDREA to see how she can help you successfully achieve your goals.

– Joshua Rosenthal, MScEd
   Founder/Director, Institute for Integrative Nutrition

CONTENTS

YOU ARE HERE

FINANCES

RELATIONSHIPS

WORK

SPIRITUAL
PRACTICE

PHYSICAL
ACTIVITY

NOURISH
YOUR BODY

CIRCLE OF LIFE

1. BEGIN HERE

This book is a simple step-by-step guide to help you manage your finances with confidence and ease as you meet the challenges to achieve your goals throughout your lifetime. Managing a balance in the financial area of your life plays a major role as you seek to keep a balance in all other areas of your life.

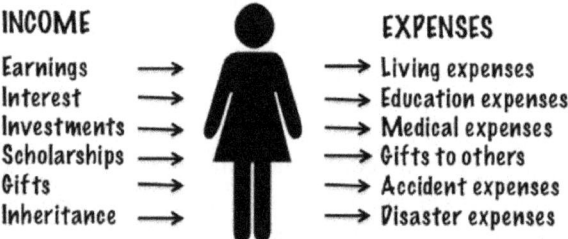

During your lifetime,
you will receive money in many ways,
and you will distribute money in many ways.

YOUR MISSION

Your mission is to enjoy a great lifestyle, but also to manage the money that comes into your life to make sure you have enough financial resources for your <u>entire lifetime</u>.

There will be times when you will not have enough money when you need it.

Expect surprises.
Be prepared.

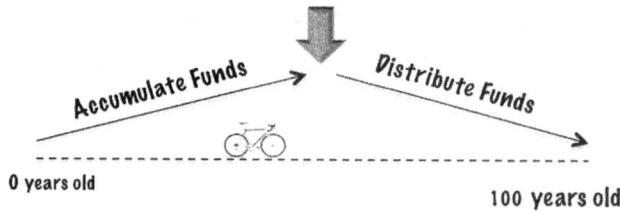

ACCUMULATION AND DISTRIBUTION

The first half of the financial journey is the time when you **accumulate** and save funds from earnings, interest and investments.

The second half of the journey is the time when you **distribute** and live on the funds that you saved.

Retirement is the point in time when you no longer receive an income from earnings and you begin to live on the funds that you saved. It is the tipping point when you shift from accumulating funds to distributing funds.

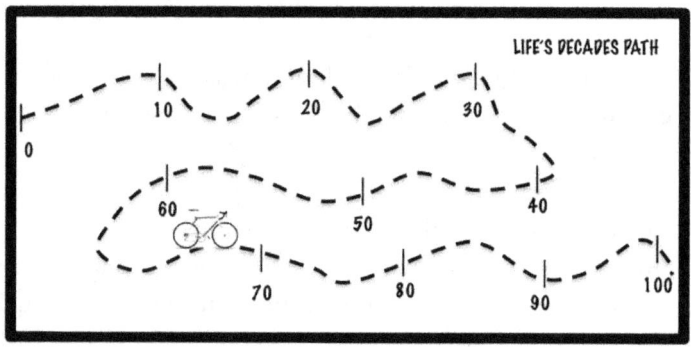

LIFE'S DECADES PATH

WILL I HAVE ENOUGH MONEY WHEN I RETIRE?

When can you plan to retire? The answer depends on what actions you take each decade of your life.

It is best to start your financial journey with a plan so you know where you are going and you have some ideas about how to get there.

The following chapters describe some basic financial guidelines and tools that you may find helpful as you build your plan.

2. THREE BASIC MONEY GUIDELINES

There are 3 powerful guidelines for positioning money. If you use them, you can speed up the process of growing your money over time.

> Compound Interest
> The Rule of 72
> Dollar-cost Averaging

Example of Compound Interest

	Sarah		Peter	
Age	Contribution	Value End of Year	Contribution	Value End of Year
19	$2,000	$2,200	$0	$0
20	$2,000	$4,620	$0	$0
21	$2,000	$7,280	$0	$0
22	$2,000	$10,210	$0	$0
23	$2,000	$13,431	$0	$0
24	$2,000	$16,974	$0	$0
25	$2,000	$20,872	$0	$0
26	$2,000	$25,159	$0	$0
27	$0	$27,675	$2,000	$2,200
28	$0	$30,442	$2,000	$4,620
29	$0	$33,487	$2,000	$7,280
30	$0	$36,835	$2,000	$10,210
31	$0	$40,519	$2,000	$13,431
32	$0	$44,571	$2,000	$16,974
33	$0	$49,028	$2,000	$20,872
34	$0	$53.930	$2,000	$25,159
35	$0	$59,323	$2,000	$29,875
36	$0	$65,256	$2,000	$35,062
37	$0	$71,781	$2,000	$40,769
38	$0	$78,960	$2,000	$47,045
39	$0	$86,856	$2,000	$53,950
40	$0	$95,541	$2,000	$61,545
41	$0	$105,095	$2,000	$69,899
42	$0	$115,605	$2,000	$79,089
43	$0	$127,165	$2,000	$89,198
44	$0	$139,882	$2,000	$100,318
45	$0	$153,870	$2,000	$112,550
46	$0	$169,257	$2,000	$126,005
47	$0	$186,183	$2,000	$140,805
48	$0	$204,801	$2,000	$157,086
49	$0	$225,281	$2,000	$174,995
50	$0	$247,809	$2,000	$194,694
51	$0	$272,590	$2,000	$216,364
52	$0	$299,849	$2,000	$240,200
53	$0	$329,834	$2,000	$266,420
54	$0	$362,834	$2,000	$295,262
55	$0	$399,099	$2,000	$326,988
56	$0	$439,009	$2,000	$361,887
57	$0	$482,918	$2,000	$400,276
58	$0	$531,201	$2,000	$442,503
59	$0	$584,321	$2,000	$488,953
60	$0	$642,753	$2,000	$540.049
61	$0	$707,028	$2,000	$596,254
62	$0	$777,731	$2,000	$658,079
63	$0	$855,504	$2,000	$726,079
64	$0	$941,054	$2,000	$800,000
65	$0	**$1,035,160**	$2,000	**$883,185**

⬆   ⬆

COMPOUND INTEREST

Compound Interest means that over time, interest earned on your money will begin to accumulate more rapidly. How can you make compound interest work for you?

First, decide what percent of your income to set aside.
Next, convert the percentage to a dollar amount.
Then, commit to save that amount each week or month.

Example of Compound Interest

Sarah is 19 and just started a new job. She makes $400 a week. She is determined to stick to her plan to save 10%, of her income, which is $40 a week. She will be able to save $2,000 a year with interest on the interest. The chart shows how Sarah's account grows with only 8 years of deposits at 10% interest.

Peter, who started later at age 27, makes deposits all his life, yet his account never grows as much as Sarah's. This is the power of compound interest over time.

How Long Will It Take To Double My Money?

Table of Returns

Interest Rate	Years to Double Your Money
1%	72
2%	36
3%	24
4%	18
5%	14
6%	12
7%	10.3
8%	9
9%	8
10%	7.2
11%	6.5
12%	6
13%	5.5
14%	5.1
15%	4.8

Example of The Rule of 72

If you save $1,000 at 4% interest, it will take you 18 years to double your money to $2,000. If you save $1,000 at 10% interest, it will double in 7.2 years!

THE RULE OF 72

The Rule of 72, which was discovered by Albert Einstein, is a guideline to determine how long it will take to double your money.

Simply divide 72 by the interest rate and that will give you the years it will take to double your investment.

For example, if you earn a 6 percent rate of return on your money, divide 72 by 6 percent. This calculation shows it will take 12 years to double your money.

$$72 \div 6 = 12$$

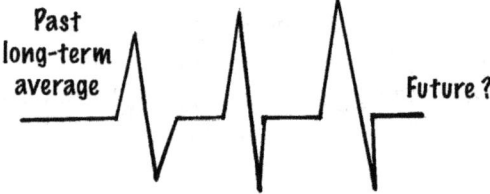

DOLLAR-COST AVERAGING

Dollar-cost averaging refers to systematically investing the same amount of money, in all your investments, on a regular fixed schedule (weekly, biweekly, or monthly).

On a regular schedule you will purchase various stocks. Some stocks will be purchased at a lower rate and some will be purchased at a higher rate, however, over time the average cost will be to your advantage.

When you automatically have payments going to your investment account, such as your 401(k), then you are making automatic investments of the same amount on a fixed time schedule.

Dollar-cost averaging was created to take the emotion out of investing. It avoids panic selling and impulse buying. It allows the investor to stick to the plan of buy low, sell high.

3. TOOLS TO HELP
YOUR SAVINGS GROW

There are several places where you can place your money during the accumulation phase so savings can grow and be available for the distribution phase later in your life.

Individual Retirement Accounts (IRAs)

401(k) Accounts

Investment Accounts

Insurance Accounts

INDIVIDUAL RETIREMENT ACCOUNTS (IRAs)

TRADITIONAL IRA
Tax-deferred Growth
- ✓ Open at any age
- ✓ Tax-deferred contributions
- ✓ When withdraw, contributions and interest are taxable
- ✓ Penalty if withdraw before 59½
- ✓ Must withdraw 10% each year after turn 70½
- ✓ $5,500 limit each year ($6,500 if you are over 50)

ROTH IRA
Tax-free Growth
- ✓ Open at any age
- ✓ Pre-paid tax contributions
- ✓ When withdraw, contributions and interest are tax-free
- ✓ Can withdraw contributions anytime
- ✓ No withdrawal requirements each year after turn 70½
- ✓ $5,500 limit each year ($6,500 if you are over 50)

401(K) RETIREMENT ACCOUNT

A 401(k) plan allows employees to save a portion of their paycheck before taxes are taken out.

Many employers will match a portion of an employee's contribution. The money your employer puts in your 401(k) for you is **free money**.

The savings can grow *tax-deferred* until the money is withdrawn. When you make a withdrawal, it will be taxed as ordinary income.

When you leave your employer. Be sure to transfer (rollover) your 401(k) to an Individual Retirement Account (IRA). You then have the option to transfer the funds from the IRA to a Roth IRA.

Special Penalty Exempt Withdrawal. If you leave your employer after you reach 55 and before you turn 59½, you may take withdrawals that are exempt from the penalty tax. Do not rollover funds from a 401(k) to an IRA before you reach 59½. If you do, the age 55 penalty-free withdrawal provision will no longer apply.

Creditor protection. Your 401(k) is a protected asset. Do not use 401(k) money to avoid bankruptcy, foreclosure, pay off debt or start a business. Only use it for your retirement.

S&P 500 (500 stocks)
The S&P 500 is an index of the 500 most widely held company stocks that people own. It is seen by many as one of the best ways to track the U.S. economy.

NASDAQ (4000 stocks)
The NASDAQ index (also called the "blue chip" index) tracks 4,000 stocks listed on the NASDAQ exchange, which are weighted towards the information technology sector.

DOW (30 stocks)
The Dow Jones Industrial Average is comprised of 30 well-known companies. Although the Dow was initially created to reflect the American industrial sector, its current components include Disney, Microsoft, Apple, Coca-Cola and Nike.

INVESTMENTS

Investments, such as stocks, mutual funds, and real estate, can also grow your money and provide you with an income.

The stock market can refer to the three major stock indices: the S&P 500, the NASDAQ Stock Market, and the Dow Jones Industrial Average

The profits that you make from these investments will be taxed in one of two ways depending how long you have held the investment.

If you held an <u>investment for greater than 12 months</u>, the **long-term capital gains tax applies,** which is 15%.

If you have held an <u>investment for less than 12 months,</u> **the short-term capital gains tax** will apply, which is usually at the rate of your marginal income tax.

Do You Know Your Marginal Tax Rate?

Are you single or married?

If you are married, are you filing together or separately?

How much income did you have for the year?

Find your Marginal Tax Rate below.

Marginal Tax Rate	Single Return	Married Joint Return	Married Separate Return
10%	$0	$0	$0
15%	$9276	$18,551	$9,276
25%	$37,651	$75,301	$37,651
28%	$91,151	$151,901	$75,951
33%	$190,151	$231,451	$115,726
35%	$413,351	$413,351	$206,676
39.6%	$415,050	$466,951 +	$233,476 +

Based on Federal Income Tax Rates for 2016

TERM VS. PERMANENT LIFE INSURANCE

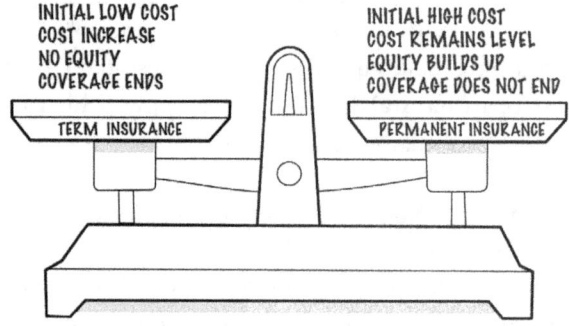

LIFE INSURANCE

There are two main types of life insurance: <u>term</u> life insurance and <u>permanent</u> life insurance. Deciding on which insurance to purchase depends on why you need it, the amount of coverage you need, what you can afford.

Term life insurance is life insurance that provides coverage for a limited period of time and at a fixed rate for that time. If the insured person dies within the period of time, the death benefit will be paid tax free to the beneficiary. If the insured does not die before that period of time, the coverage would end and the policy owner may then have the option to again obtain coverage with new conditions and a different payment.

Term insurance is used primarily for income replacement for such things as paying off debts, the mortgage, living expenses for several years, education for dependents, funeral costs, etc. The objective is that when the insured dies, the beneficiaries would be able to take care of the expenses.

Permanent life insurance (also called full life, whole life, universal life, variable universal life) is life insurance that guarantees coverage at fixed premiums for the entire lifetime of the insured, as long as the policy owner continues to pay the premium (payment) and does not allow the policy to lapse. The permanent life insurance premium is usually much more costly than the term life insurance premium. The reason term insurance costs are considerably lower is because term insurance may expire without paying out, however, permanent insurance must eventually pay out.

4. HOW MONEY IS TAXED

There are two main types of money: *tax-free* money and *taxable* money. *Tax-free* money is money that you do not have to pay taxes on when you receive it. *Taxable* money is money that you must pay taxes on when you receive it.

TAX-FREE MONEY

FREE MONEY

When you receive money, for example from your family for your birthday, or holidays, or perhaps someone gives you money, that money is *free* money. You do not pay tax on it.

You may also receive free money from your **employer's 401(k) matching funds benefit**. When you enroll in your employer's 401(k) fund, you will be asked to specify what percentage of your salary is to be regularly taken from your earnings (before taxes are taken out) and automatically placed in your 401(k). If the company will match up to 5 percent, you may elect to have 5 percent of each paycheck go to your account and the company will match that amount. If you elect to have 10 percent of your paycheck deposited to the account, the company will still match only 5 percent. *Note: you will pay taxes on all of the 401(k) money when you withdraw it. You will be taxed on your original contribution, the matching funds, and the interest.*

TAX-FREE MONEY

Tax-free money also includes money you will <u>not</u> pay taxes on when you <u>withdraw</u> and receive the funds.

When you contribute money into a **Roth Individual Retirement Account (Roth IRA)** or **Life Insurance Policy**, the money will accumulate and earn interest. When you withdraw the funds, **your original contributions and all interest will be tax-free income** to you.

TAXABLE MONEY

TAX-DEFERRED MONEY

Tax-deferred money is money (earnings) that you did not pay taxes on when you earned it. Instead of paying taxes on the earnings, you took the option to defer paying the taxes and to invest the money in a 401(k) or a Traditional IRA. However, when you withdraw the funds, you will pay taxes on the contributions and the interest earned.

If you withdraw funds before you turn 59½, you will pay a penalty and taxes on the amount withdrawn.

After you turn 70½ years old, you will be required to withdraw 10% from your account by April 1 each year. The money withdrawn each year will be taxable.

* * *

ALL OTHER TAXABLE MONEY

Taxable money refers to all other money you receive:
- ✓ Earned Income
- ✓ Profits on Investments
- ✓ Stocks
- ✓ Mutual Funds
- ✓ Real Estate

For profits you made on investments that you held for more than 12 months, you pay a  long-term gains tax, which for most people is currently 15%.

For profits you made on investments that you held for less than 12 months, you pay a short-term gains tax, which is currently the same rate as your current income tax rate.

5. YOUR SOCIAL SECURITY STRATEGY

S ocial Security is a program that collects payroll taxes out of your work paycheck, and then provides you with a monthly Social Security retirement payment later in life.

Your strategy is to have your monthly Social Security payment be an important supplement to your savings and any pensions, rather than relying on it to be a primary source of income during your retirement years.

When you reach age 66 or 67 depending on the year you were born, you will be eligible to receive a full monthly Social Security payment (based on your employment history) for the rest of your life.

You may elect to begin your payments as early as 62, but at 75% of the full amount.

Or you may elect to delay payments until you are age 70, and receive as much as 32% more than the full amount.

In addition, the monthly amount may increase each January, based on the cost-of-living adjustments (COLAs), which are determined each October by the Social Security Administration.

Task 1. Become eligible for Social Security benefits

You must work in a Social Security covered job for at least 10 years. More specifically, you need to earn 40 credits. You can earn up to 4 credits a year by earning a minimum dollar amount.

Earn four credits a year for 10 years, and you will have earned the 40 credits required to be fully insured and eligible for benefits when you reach your 60s.

WHEN TO FILE DECISIONS

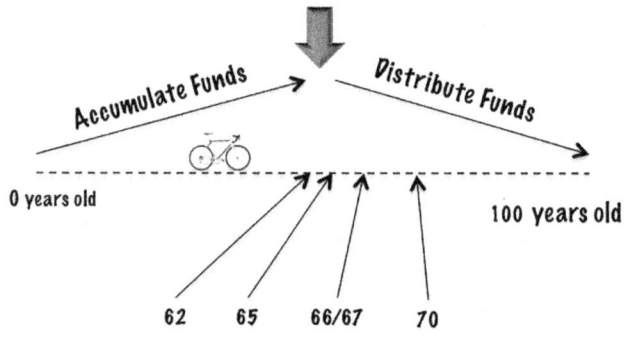

62
Do I file for early Social Security payments?
Do I file for spousal benefits?

65
I must remember to file for Medicare 3 months before
my birthday.

66 or 67
What year am I entitled to full Social Security
monthly payments?

Years between 66/67 and 70
Each year I wait to file, my benefits increase by 8%.

70
Remember to sign up a month before my birthday for
the most Social Security benefits! Yeah!

Task 2. Plan when to begin to receive Social Security benefits

One of the most important decisions you will make is when to begin to receive your monthly income from Social Security.

At age 62, you are eligible to receive benefits, however payments will be at 75% of your full payment. You will receive even less if you are working. For every $2 you earn over $1,310 per month (for 2016), $1 in benefits will be withheld.

At age 66 (for people born between 1943 and 1954) or at age 67 (for people born after 1954), you are eligible to receive your full monthly payment.

At age 70, you *must* begin receiving your monthly payments.

For each year after age 66/67 that you delay the start of your benefits, your benefit will increase by 8% per year up to the age of 70. You can apply anytime between your 66th and 70th birthdays and receive a prorated credit for the delay. If you wait to begin benefits until age 70, your full payment may increase by as much as 32% (4 years times 8%).

✳ ✳ ✳

An important long-term planning issue is whether you should plan to apply for early benefits if you plan to work. If possible, it is suggested that you wait until full retirement age to apply for your benefits. After you reach full retirement age, you can earn any amount from working and no benefits will be withheld.

Go to www.socialsecurity.gov. Click on Retirement Planner to learn more about the effect of early or delayed retirement. You can also use the Savvy Social Security planning calculators.

Example of Your Earnings Record

Years You Worked	Your Taxed Social Security Earnings	Your Taxed Medicare Earnings
1990	654	654
1991	1,592	1,592
1992	2,854	2,854
1993	4,678	4,678
1994	6,367	6,367
1995	7,923	7,923
1996	9,985	9,985
1997	13,095	13,095
1998	16,232	16,232
1999	19,252	19,252
2000	22,240	22,240
2001	24,543	24,543
2002	26,341	26,341
2003	28,412	28,412
2004	30,970	30,970
2005	33,253	33,253
2006	35,799	35,799
2007	38,342	38,342
2008	40,065	40,065
2009	40,191	40,191
2010	41,790	41,790
2011	43,768	43,768
2012	45,718	45,718
2013	Not yet recorded	

Task 3. Track your Social Security Statement of Earnings

To request your Social Security Summary of Earnings and verify that the income amounts are correct for each year, go online to www.socialsecurity.gov/myaccount. You also may call 800.772.1213.

Task 4. Obtain your Estimated Benefits for your retirement

When you turn 62, your earnings for the highest 35 years are tallied, a formula is applied, and your primary insurance amount (PIA) is determined. It is the amount you will receive each month if you apply for benefits at your full retirement age (66/67). You should receive your Statement of Benefits Summary sheet or you will be able to view it online.

The predetermined amount will vary depending on when you actually apply for benefits, however the relatively accurate estimate will allow you to build the rest of your retirement plan around that amount of income.

May you grow up to be righteous,
May you grow up to be true,
May you always know the truth
And see the light surrounding you.
May you always be courageous,
Stand upright and be strong,
And may you stay forever young.
~ Song lyrics by Bob Dylan

Task 5. Apply for Social Security benefits when the time is right

Plan ahead of time when you want to begin receiving benefits. To learn more about your personal account, go online to www.socialsecurity.gov, or call them at 800.772.1213. or go to your local Social Security office. Use the Social Security locator at www.ssa.gov for the address, driving directions, and hours.

Task 6. *Consider timing for spousal benefits*

If you are married, you may be eligible for spousal benefits independent of your personal Social Security account. Note, you must specifically ask to discuss spousal benefits.

Example: Married person with little or no earnings history
Mary, a married person with little or no earnings history, can receive a spousal benefit equal to half of the monthly payment received by Bob, her working spouse. When Bob applies for his Social Security benefit, Mary can also apply for her spousal benefit. If she is full retirement age when she applies, she will receive an amount equal to half of Bob's monthly payment. If she applies at age 62, she will receive an amount equal to 35% of his monthly payment.

Example: Spousal benefits for two high earners
Linda has worked in a high-paying position and files for her benefits. After she files, and when her husband Tom turns 66, he may apply for spousal benefits or for his full payment benefit. He will receive whichever is the highest amount.

Task 7. Consider divorced spousal benefits

If you were married at least 10 years and are now divorced, and you are unmarried, you may receive spousal benefits based on your ex-spouses work record. He needs to be at least 62 years old, however he does not need to apply for his benefit in order for you to receive your benefits. You do not need to know where he is or his earnings history. All you need is proof that you were married and divorced.

Task 8. Consider widow/widower spousal benefits

If both of you are receiving Social Security benefits, and one spouse dies, then the deceased spouse's benefit will stop. You may then switch over to your survivor benefit, if it is higher. If you are over full retirement age when you claim it, you will receive 100% of the deceased benefit. Note that you will go from two incomes to one income. Life insurance or other liquid assets will help fill this gap.

Task 9. Estimate how your Social Security will be taxed

Your Social Security benefits may be taxed. How much your benefits will be taxed depends on how much other income you receive, such as, earned income, pensions, investments, tax-free municipal bonds.

Up to 50% of your benefits will be taxed if your combined income (your modified adjusted income, half of your Social Security benefits, and tax-exempt interest) is between $25,000 and $34,000 for those filing as an individual, and between $32,000 and $44,000 for those filing a joint return.

Up to 85% of your benefits may be taxed if you are married filing jointly & your income exceeds $44,000, or you are single and your income exceeds $34,000. If you are married filing separately, 85% of your benefits will be taxed no matter how much other income you may have.

It's easy to understand
what's going on with your money.

6. TOOLS TO MANAGE YOUR FINANCES

Thanks to the Internet, you are able to view your financial accounts and manage your transactions online from the comfort of your home or anywhere in the world.

MINT.COM

Mint.com offers a fantastic money-management tool that lets you have a complete clear view of all your finances in one place: bill pay, credit score, budgeting, investing. It is ideal for people who don't want to spend time balancing a checkbook or checking multiple financial institutions' websites.

Mint allows you to have a comprehensive, quick insight into your finances from your computer, mobile phone and/or tablet.

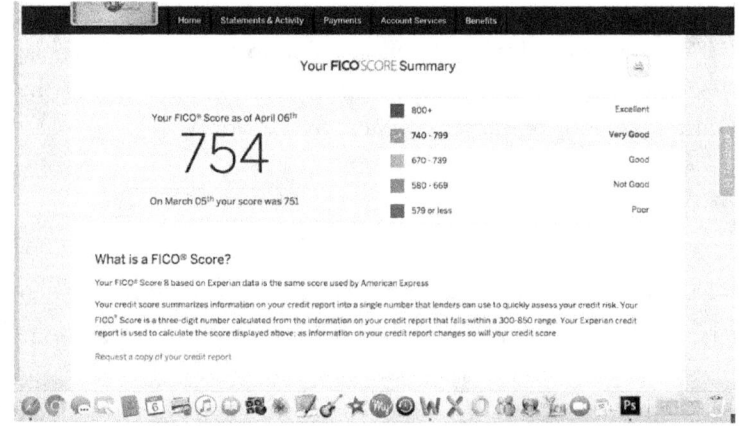

YOUR CREDIT REPORT

Your credit report is one of the most important tools you can use to maintain your financial security and credit rating.

Now several banks offer you the ability to view your credit information for free through your account. Your credit report is also available for free through your account with Mint.com. Check with your bank or open an account with Mint.com and start tracking your credit score and credit report.

Your credit score, which is a 3-digit number based on the information on your credit report, is a measure of your credit worthiness and will usually play a large role when you apply for credit. It can determine the kind of loan that you qualify for, how much credit you qualify for, and what your interest rate will be. A higher credit score can save you hundreds or thousands of dollars.

Employers, property renting companies, cell phone companies, insurance companies, may also use your score. There are 3 credit bureaus that maintain your credit report information: Experian, Equifax and TransUnion.

The 5 ways to keep your credit score in great shape are:
- ✓ Always pay your bills on time
- ✓ Keep your credit balances below 30% of your total credit limits
- ✓ Keep your accounts open and in good standing to establish a long credit history
- ✓ Do not apply for credit with too many companies and have too many inquiries
- ✓ Check your credit regularly through your bank, Mint.com, or at www.annualcreditreport.com

If you do not know where you are going,
every road will get you nowhere.
~ Henry Kissinger

7. HOW TO BUILD
YOUR FINANCIAL PLAN

Now that you are familiar with the basic guidelines and tools to manage finances, the next task is to chart out a course for your financial journey and build your financial plan.

Something magical happens when you have a plan. You know you can reach your goals. Follow the steps and stick to your plan to achieve your lifetime goals.

Preparation

Step 1. Commit to be an investor

Step 2. Pay yourself first

Step 3. Set up an emergency fund

Step 4. Define your dreams and goals

Step 5. Speed up achieving your goals

Step 6. Know where and how to invest your money

Step 7. Have a retirement strategy

Step 8. Review your financial plan each year

Example Of My Numbers

1. INCOME

#1 Job	$800/wk	$3,200/mo	$38,400/yr
#2 Job	$150/wk	$600/mo	$7,200/yr

2. LIVING EXPENSES

What I really need for basic monthly living expenses:

1. Rent or mortgage	$1000
2. Utilities (electricity, gas, water, phone)	$300
3. Food, Household	$510
4. Transportation	$605
5. Insurance	$300
Total per month	$2,715
Total per year (monthly x 12)	$32,580

The total $2,715 per month ($32,580 per year)
Is how much I need to be financially secure.

3. DEBTS

Chase Visa:	$3,890	$76 per month	9.99%
Capital One:	$2,480	$78 per month	14.9%

Preparation

Before going to Step 1, take a moment to prepare 2 items: a list of your numbers and a list of your accounts.

Know Your Numbers
If you want to manage your finances, you can begin by measuring where you currently are and how much it will take to reach your goals.

1. Income
Make a list of all of your current sources of income.
Think about ways and how much your income will grow.

2. Living Expenses
Calculate what you really need for basic monthly living expenses:

1. Rent or mortgage _____
2. Utilities (electricity, gas, water, phone)_____
3. Food   _____
4. Transportation   _____
5. Insurance   _____
Total per month   _____
Total per year (monthly x 12) _____

The total monthly amount is how much you truly need to be financially secure. (The US national average for basic annual expenses is $34,668.)

3. Debt
List all your debts. For each debt list the total owed, monthly payment, and interest percentage.

Example Of My Financial Accounts

1. Checking   Chase   12345678 $1847.60

2. Savings   (Emergency Account)
               Chase   910111213 $2,355.30
               Monthly payment $100
               % .01

3. Roth IRA   (Retirement Account)
               Fidelity   1415161718 $6,588.90
               Monthly payment $160
               % 4

4. 401(k)   (Retirement Account)
               American Funds 1920212 $14,107.56
               Monthly payment $160
               % 9.2 (last year)

Know Where Your Financial Accounts Are Located
List all your financial institutions where you have accounts. For each account list the institution name, account number, total amount, any monthly payments, and interest it is earning.

Checking

Emergency Savings Account

Retirement Accounts
    Roth IRA

    Traditional IRA

    401(k)

Mortgage (or Home Savings) Account

Car Loan (or Car Savings) Account

Education Account

Insurance

Other Account(s)

I commit to be an investor.

I commit to save 10% of every dollar.

Step 1. Commit to be an investor

One of the most important *financial* decisions you can make at the very start of your financial journey is to decide to be an *investor (not a consumer)* to achieve your goals.

Make the commitment to yourself that each time you receive a paycheck (or money from any source), you will invest at least 10% of it.

It does not matter how much money you earn – $1,000, $10,000, $100,000 or $1 million a year. Put some money aside by investing it, otherwise you will lose it all.

Example of How To Pay Yourself First Automatically

Mary makes $50,000 a year. She wants to save 10% a year. That is $5,000 a year.

Mary has 5% of her paycheck ($2,500 after taxes) *automatically* deducted and deposited into her Emergency Fund account at CapitalOne360, which pays 1.5% interest.

Mary also *automatically* contributes 5% of her income ($50,000 times .05% = $2,500) to her 401(k) account. As part of the employer sponsored 401(k) plan at work, her employer will match her contributions up to 5% of her income. The matching $2,500 is free money to her. At the end of the year, her 401(k) account will be at $5,000.

At the end of the first year, Mary has kept her promise to herself to save 10% and the total of her accounts show $7,500!

Step 2. Pay yourself first

The best way to pay yourself first is to _automatically_ save a recommended 10% of your gross income (income before taxes). This is doable, regardless of how little or how much you make.

When you are tempted to spend the amount you are setting aside, resist. Adjust your living standards, if needed. Just keep reminding yourself to focus on achieving your goals, sticking to your plan, and relying on the power of compound interest.

EMERGENCIES
- → Health care expenses
- → Job loss coverage
- → Car breakdown expenses
- → Disaster expenses

BE PREPARED WITH YOUR
EMERGENCY FUND

Step 3. Set up an emergency fund

The first account you must have is an **Emergency Fund**. Put money into this fund before you pay debt or put money in a 401(k).

Why do you need an emergency supply of cash on hand? You may have a health issue, or you may be displaced from your job. You need peace of mind that you will have a roof over your head, food and the bills will be paid.

Earlier in the section you determined the amount of money you need to feel secure each month. The best amount to target for an emergency fund would be enough to cover your monthly basic expenses for 6 to 12 months. Have an account at an FDIC insured bank. Focus on making it happen and you will have peace of mind that you are covered when an emergency occurs.

No one knows how long he or she will live. No one knows what fortunes or misfortunes they will encounter along the timeline of their journey. Your best strategy is to be prepared ahead for all adventures that you will experience.

Examples of Dreams Converted To Goals

Dream 1: Take a vacation to France
Goal: Take a 2 week vacation to Paris, France in April
           Stay at Airbnb, 2 trips to nearby areas, train pass
Time: 1 year from now
Funds: $2,400
Save: $200 per month ($50 per week)

Dream 2: Have $1.5 million retirement account when age 65
Goal: Build a retirement savings of $1,500,000 over 30
           years (between ages 35-65)
Time: Build account over 30 years
Funds: $1,500,000
Save: $1,493 per month ($348 per week)

Contact Financial Advisor for best current interest rates
Invest now using one of the following compound interest
investment options:
- Invest $2161 each month at 4% interest
- Invest $1493 each month at 6% interest
- Invest $1006 each month at 8% interest
- Invest $664 each month at 10% interest

Step 4. Define your dreams and goals

✓ **Identify your dream**
Make a list of your dreams. For example, create a college savings, take a special vacation, buy a home.

✓ **Convert the dream to a goal**
Next, convert each dream to a goal by providing more detail and a timeframe. For example, buy a home for under $200,000, located in an income tax-free state, within 10 years.

✓ **Determine the amount of money needed**
Determine how much money is needed to achieve each goal. Be sure to consider all additional costs.

✓ **Calculate the amount to save each month**
Calculate the amount of money to save each month and for how much time.

✓ **Invest to achieve the goal**
Invest the amount needed each month and watch the amount grow until you achieve the goal.

Step 5. Speed up achieving your goals

Save More

Save more by promising yourself that if you receive a raise, or a bonus, you will take a portion of that increase, say 3% or 5%, and invest that money.

You can also save more if you opt to send your monthly mortgage payment and include a second check, which is a prepayment of the principal for the next month's mortgage payment. For example, if your monthly mortgage payment was $1500 and your next month's principal was $250, you would send in both checks. Do this each month and you could reduce your 30 year mortgage to 15 years.

Earn More

Take on an extra job. Make an effort to invest in yourself by learning new skills. Take courses that add to your personal development and your value. Start to get paid for your value.

Reduce fees

Find lower interest fee charges for your home, car, credit cards, investments. Reduce auto loan fees. Reduce hidden fees in mutual funds and find low cost index funds to invest in.

Reduce taxes

Pay attention to 3 taxes: Income Tax, Long-term Capital Gains Tax, and Short-term Capital Gains Tax. Grow your investments in a Roth IRA so in the future you will access the funds and interest tax-free. Invest in ways (401(k), IRA, annuity) that allow you to defer taxes. Hold your investments for one year and a day to qualify for the long-term gains tax rate. Consider moving to a state with less or no state income tax (AZ, FL, NV, NH, SD, TN, TX, WA, WY).

What Is Your Tolerance Level for Risk?

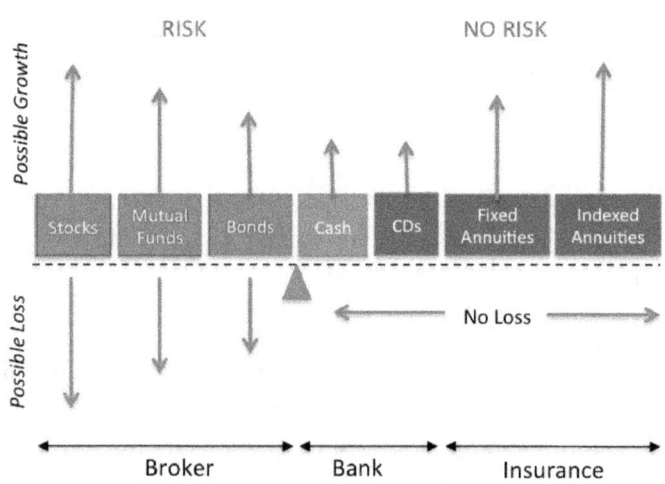

Step 6. Know where and how to invest your money

Knowing where to invest really depends on your **goals, needs, stage in life**, and your **risk level.** Knowing how to invest your money refers to knowing in what proportions to allocate your money.

More secure places to invest your money include: cash, certificates of deposit (CDs), bonds, pensions, annuities. Places that have risk include: stocks, real estate, commodities (gold, silver, oil, coffee, cotton, etc.), and collectibles. Each option has a different risk level. You will need to determine your risk comfort level.

Asset Allocation refers to the concept of spreading your money across different (diversified) types of investments so over time you reduce your risk, but you can also enhance your upside returns. You want to diversify your investments over various asset classes and across markets. Diversifying helps you avoid letting your emotions mess up your asset allocation plan. Dollar-cost averaging, as previously discussed, is how you execute asset allocation <u>over time</u>.

A financial advisor can review your portfolio and create an asset allocation to fit your goals, needs, stage in life, and risk level. To find an advisor, go to <u>www.findanadvisor.com</u>.

WHEN TO FILE DECISIONS

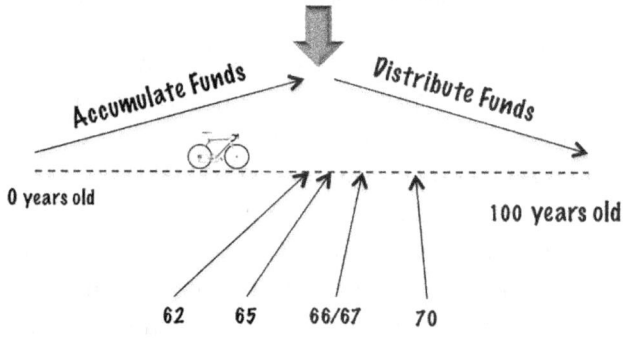

62
Do I file for early Social Security payments?
Do I file for spousal benefits?

65
I must remember to file for Medicare 3 months before
my birthday.

66 or 67
What year am I entitled to full Social Security
monthly payments?

Years between 66/67 and 70
Each year I wait to file, my benefits increase by 8%.

70
Remember to sign up a month before my birthday for
the most Social Security benefits! Yeah!

Step 7. Have a retirement strategy

Your goal is to have an income during your entire retirement - the time when you no longer receive an income from earnings. Your strategy is to:

A. Start early to save for retirement.
The earlier you start saving, the more time your money has to grow.

B. Plan to have multiple sources of income.
Social Security, Pension, Savings, 401(k), Roth and Traditional IRA, Annuity, Life Insurance, Secure Investments and Risk/Growth Investments

C. Determine at what age to retire.

D. Have a vision for retirement.
Determine what you want to do for your next 20 or 30 years.

E. Determine if adjustments need to be made now.
Do you have lower daily living expenses so you can have more money for fun activities or travel?

F. Limit fees and taxes to save more for retirement.

G. Determine if you need to *or* want to work longer.

H. Adjust asset allocation.
Look at your goals and at the economy to see if you should tone down stock exposure and have other more conservative financial products that ensure your money lasts your lifetime.

I. Build a good relationship with a financial advisor.
Your advisor can help ensure that your strategy is to your advantage.

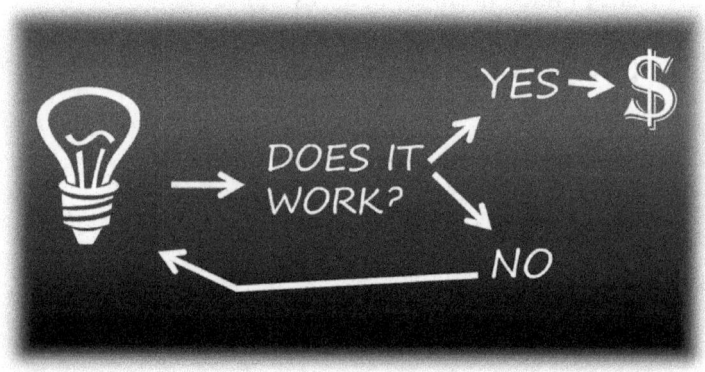

Step 8. Review your financial plan each year

Schedule an annual review with your advisor to discuss what has occurred along your financial journey, and what are your near-term and long-term expectations.

Gather all the information and discuss your progress, goals, issues and questions. Your advisor will be happy to provide you with solution options, find answers to your questions, and provide you with the information you need to be able to continue to manage your finances with confidence and ease.

Each person is on an individual journey. With laser focus, you will be able to take action and achieve what you set out to do. The following resources may help you along the way.

1. Learn about economic principles and how the economy works: www.economicprinciples.org

2. How to find an advisor: http://findanadvisor.napfa.org/home.aspx

3. Check the fees on your 401(k) plan: http://americasbest401k.com/401k-fee-checker

4. Find out how much future income you can have for only $300 per month: www.lifetime.com

5. Discover more about the S.T.A.R.T. (Save Today and Retire Tomorrow) program sponsored by the state of Florida (www.MyFloridaCFO.com/YMM).

Example Goals On Your Financial Journey

Ages 0 – 9

Obtain my social security number.

Learn to save.

Learn gratitude.

Learn to share with others.

Ages 10 – 19

Save gifts received on birthdays, holidays, graduation.

Open a savings account.

Secure my first job and save wages.

Open a checking account.

Save 10% from my wages.

Learn to manage money for college fees and living expenses.

Begin to track my credit score.

Ages 20 – 29

Educate myself on personal finance.

Create and maintain a savings plan and a spending plan.

Find a financial advisor.

Create a Personal Trust for my car, home, accounts.

Continue to track my credit score.

Save 10% from my wages.

Have an emergency account.

Save matching amount in company 401(k).

Start long-term retirement account ($2000 per year).

Plan debt repayment for student loans.

Have life insurance (debts, mortgage, living, kids' education).

Start a side job for extra income to achieve goals.

Ages 30 – 39
Purchase a home.
Maintain a budget and save 10% from wages.

Ages 40 – 49
Maintain a budget and save 10% from wages.

Ages 50 – 59½
Maintain a budget and save 10% from wages.

Ages 60 – 69
Determine best year to file for social security benefits.
File for Medicare at 65.
Check allocation of investments each year.
Update Will and Trust.
Determine a legacy plan.
Have a plan to protect assets.
Plan for possible long-term care.

Ages 70 - 79
File for maximum Social Security benefits.
Begin to withdraw 10% from 401(k) after turn 70½.
Begin to withdraw 10% from IRA accounts after turn 70½.
Check allocation of investments each year.

Ages 80 +
Check allocation of investments each year.

8. HOW NOT TO GET LOST ON YOUR JOURNEY

There are many ways you can get lost or distracted as you travel along your financial journey. Here are 8 of the ways you could fail at your mission.

> Do Nothing
> No Plan
> Procrastinate
> Small Leaks
> Instant Gratification
> Interest Illusions
> Get Rich Quickly
> Delayed Taxes

DO NOTHING

After reading everything in this book you may be tempted to *do nothing*. If you do not overcome the feeling to *do nothing*, then nothing will change for you.

You can avoid this danger by being willing to act - build your plan, set up your savings accounts, ensure you are paying yourself first with 10% of all money that you receive, live within your means, think before you spend.

NO PLAN

If you do not have a plan, and you do not implement that plan, then you will run out of money before your journey ends.

You can easily avoid this danger by simply building a plan and sticking to it.

People don't plan to fail.
They fail to plan.

PROCRASTINATE

Time has a huge effect on your investment. You can start at any age, however starting as young as possible puts you at a greater advantage. It is never too late to begin.

SMALL LEAKS

Be aware of small expenses that add up over time: daily purchases of beverages (coffee, sodas, waters, beers, power drinks), candy, cigarettes, lunches or dinners out, pizzas out, newspapers, magazines, lottery tickets.

To avoid the temptation of small leaks, look closely at all your regular small expenses and see where you can save.

Learn to cook great meals at home, prepare healthy lunches to take to work.

Plan ahead and make clothing purchases during annual sales. Have clothing that can be washed and limit dry cleaning expenses.

Possible leaks include: phone fees, banking fees, entertainment fees (cable, internet, movie tickets, concert tickets), sports fees (gym, golf, tennis, biking), transportation expenses (gas, insurance, repairs, maintenance).

INSTANT GRATIFICATION

You may be tempted to use credit cards to purchase all sorts of expensive toys along your journey. Debt can end up being a major payment out of your budget. It can feel like a financial anchor chained to your leg. Resist your desire for instant gratification.

The way to avoid this danger is to think before you spend. Ask yourself if you really need the item or is it just a temporary desire? The feeling of financial freedom can be more gratifying than owning one more "thing."

Spend only what is in your bank account, not what is in your credit limit. Spend less than you earn. Don't buy on impulse.

If you are already in debt, stop all charging now. Then, you are free to focus on only paying off the current debt and on saving for your future.

Example of How to Be Clear About the Cost of Interest

John wants to purchase a boat for $43,000. A 10-year loan would be at 7.75% interest rate. The monthly payment would be about $520. However, other costs for insurance, maintenance, fuel, and moorage would be about $800 per month. Over the 10 years the boat would actually cost John almost $97,000!

In comparison, John calculated that he could join a boat rental company for now or if he put the same $800 a month into an investment (that does not get taxed) and averages a 12% interest return, he would have a savings of over $180,000. If he invested the funds now, he could pay cash for a boat at a later time.

INTEREST ILLUSIONS

When you are considering the purchase of an item on credit, make sure you understand the real costs of the purchase.

GET RICH QUICKLY

Get rich schemes, such as gambling, purchasing lottery tickets, multi-level marketing schemes, and many other offers have ruined many a family.

To help protect you against get-rich-quick tactics, follow the simple guidelines to invest in things that you are familiar with:

- ✓ Invest in what you know.
- ✓ Invest in things you trust.
- ✓ Invest in things you understand.
- ✓ Invest in things that have been around for decades.

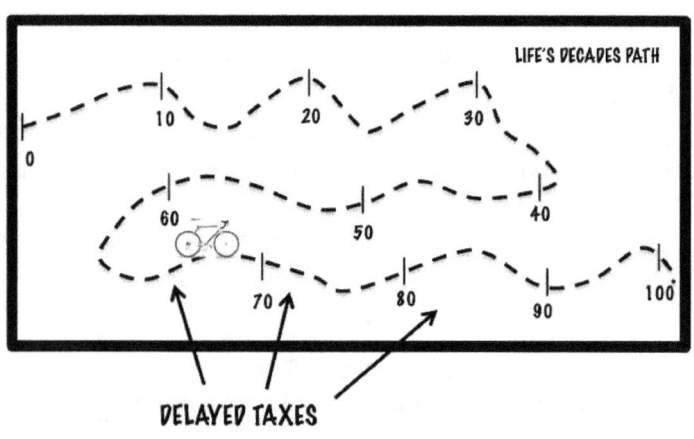

DELAYED TAXES

Throughout your journey you may be storing your retirement funds in one or more tax-qualified retirement accounts, such as a 401(k) or a Traditional IRA. These plans do not avoid taxes, they *delay* taxes.

There are 4 areas to pay attention to when it comes to tax-qualified retirement accounts:

1. Taxation
2. Access
3. Distribution
4. Distribution After Death

1. Taxation on Tax-qualified Accounts

You may want to only contribute the amount that your employer will match each year. The employer contribution is free money to you. If your employer will match 5%, then save 5%. When you retire and take a distribution, you will pay taxes on the amount withdrawn from the 401(k).

2. Access to Tax-Qualified Accounts *(59½ Solution)*

You may access your tax-qualified account, such as your 401(k) when you are 59½ years old, however, you will owe federal and state income taxes at your current tax bracket. If you access your money before you reach the age of 59½, you have to pay income tax plus an additional 10% penalty.

3. Distribution of Tax-Qualified Accounts *(70½ Solution)*

When you retire from a company you may be required to move your account from the company sponsored 401(k) to a Traditional IRA. You may not keep amounts in your Traditional IRA indefinitely.

By April 1 after the year you reach age 70½ you <u>must</u> begin taking a distribution from your tax-qualified retirement account, whether you need the money or not. The required minimum distribution for any year after the year you reach 70½ must be made by December 31 of that later year.

The company that manages your plan will contact you as to the amount that you are required to withdraw. There are also government websites that offer calculators for you to estimate the required minimum distribution you must withdraw.

If you fail to make the required withdrawal for a specific year or if distributions are less than the required minimum distribution, you may have to pay a 50% excise tax on the amount not distributed, as required.

4. After Death Distribution of Tax-Qualified Accounts

The worst place to have money when you die is in a tax-qualified account. Let's take a look at what happens to money left in a tax-qualified plan at the time of death.

If the deceased is married, then the money passes on to the spouse and there are no taxation issues. However, if that spouse remarries, the account will be heavily taxed at the death of the second spouse.

If the deceased is not married, the entire account is treated as income paid in that year and gets taxed at the appropriate tax rate.

Example of After Death Distribution

If Ronald has a tax-qualified account with $1,000,000 at the time of his death, the account would be hit with a $350,000 federal tax (top tax rate). If it were in a state with a 9% income tax, there would be an additional $90,000 state income tax collected. A total of $440,000 in taxes will be due immediately when he dies.

ABOUT THE AUTHOR

ANDREA ADAMS
HHC, CHC, AADP

Andrea Adams is an author, wealth counselor, and certified health coach. She is passionate about providing simple step-by-step guidelines so each person is able to manage the financial area of life with clarity, confidence, and ease throughout their lifetime.

Andrea, who for over 25 years developed strategic business plans for Fortune 500 companies and leading companies in Europe, now offers strategic financial and life planning services to young adults in Palm Beach Gardens, Florida. She also hosts *Women, Wine and Wealth* coaching sessions for women of all ages.

REVIEWS

Clear and easy to understand information on money and finance

At last, so clear and easy to understand information on money and finance! Yes, this book is great for young adults about to start their financial journey, but it is also very informative for anyone at any stage of their financial journey. This book is indeed loaded with all the important financial information you need to know. Maybe you are wondering what is the best way to save and invest? How much to contribute toward retirement? Or what is the difference between Roth and Traditional IRA? Or you want to know more about investments including stocks, mutual funds and real estate? You might also need to know the tax effect of your financial decisions? This book answered all those questions and much more!

Learn about money to make more money!

This is an outstanding book that teaches important finance and money basics for all ages. I found the short chapters and summary lessons very helpful. I think that whether you are starting late or beginning early, every reader will learn important money lessons that should be taught in school.

Excellent starter book for teenagers

Excellent starter book for teenagers. Straight forward, easy to read, and encapsulates all the basics for financial knowledge throughout one's life-journey. Highly recommended!

Practical Guide and Planner

The perfect gift for young people to understand and plan their future financial security.

MY FINANCIAL JOURNEY NOTES

MY FINANCIAL JOURNEY